Elements

Elements

EARTH, AIR, WATER, FIRE, COLORADO AND BEYOND

ROSEMARY BERGSTROM

Copyright © 2016 by Rosemary Bergstrom

All rights reserved. This book or any portion thereof
may not be reproduced or used in any manner whatsoever
without the express written permission of the publisher
except for the use of brief quotations in a book review.

Printed in the United States of America
Wooden Pants Publishing

Book Design
Jennifer Schafer

Photographs
Rosemary Bergstrom & Michael Bergstrom

Back Cover Photo
Rocky Mountain National Park, Estes Park, Colorado

ISBN-13: 978-0-9973535-4-9

DEDICATION

To my guardian angel and my very best friend.

CONTENTS

PREFACE

EARTH — 1

- LANDSCAPES — 2
- PLAINSWOMAN — 3
- GARDEN — 4
- LIVING ON THE PLAINS — 5
- EARTH TO EARTH — 6
    - I. Patrick Is under the Lilies — A Memory — 6
    - II. In Memoriam — 7
    - III. The Wall — 8
    - IV. The New Guard — 9
- THE MYSTERY OF PEDAGOGY — 10
    - I. Classroom Notes — 10
    - II. Herding Cats — 11
- ON THE ROAD — 12
- AUTUMN JOURNEY — 14
- MUSHROOMS AFTER RAIN — 15
- SEASONILLUSION — 16
- RECONCILIATION — 17
- CHILDREN — 18
    - I. Guardian Angels — 18
    - II. Too Much Imagination — 19
- LEFT BEHIND — 20
- A POST-MODERN GEOGRAPHY — 21
- LETTING GO — 22
- LEFTOVERS — 23

AIR — 25

- PASTORAL FANTASY — 26
    - I. Allegro — 26
    - II. Andante — 26
    - III. Presto Agitato — 27
- SALOME IN GRAY — 28
- ETCHING — 29
- NIGHTCALL — 30
- SUNLIGHT — 31
- NEW YEAR — 32

EPHEMERA	33
THE MORNING WIND	34
ECONOMY	35
RAPTOR	36
EREMITE	37
CHANSONS POUR LES OISEAUX (SONGS FOR THE BIRDS)	*38*
I. Dawn	38
II. Blackbirds	38
III. Collage	39
IV. Nightfall	39
V. Argument	40
VI. Lament	40
VII. Homecoming	41
SMOKE	42
WINGDOM	43

WATER   45

LIKE WATER	46
THE THING WITH FEATHERS	47
SHAPE SHIFTING	48
I. Morning Fog	48
II. Frost	49
III. Trapped	49
LETTER TO SYLVIA	50
WHERE I LIVE	51
DREAM WHORLS	52
COQUINA BEACH	53
CANYONS	54
ROARING RIVER	55
BIG THOMPSON	56
WATERS	57
REDWING MARSH	58

FIRE   59

THE FIRE OF PASSION	60
I. Dancers	60
II. Dimensions	61
III. The Lover: A Villanelle	62
IV. Obsession	63
V. Esse Machina Amorata	64

THE POETICS OF FIRE	65
I. Fire	65
II. Broken Dialog	65
III. Disparate Poets	65
IV. Writing Poetry	66
V. Coffeehouse Casualties	66
THE POLITICS OF FIRE	67
I. Conundrum	67
II. Street Scene	68
III. Terror by Other Names	69
IV. Common Denominator	70
V. Anthem	71
THE WARMTH OF FIRE	72
I. The Letter	72
II. Home for Christmas	73

QUINTESSENCE   75

RAINBOW	76
TARANTULA	77
CELESTIAL ENCOUNTERS	78
I. Journey	78
II. Full Moon	79
III. New Moon	79
BROKEN MIRROR	80
IMMANENCE	82
TIME	84
REFLECTIONS	85
PERSPECTIVE	86
COMING HOME	88

PREFACE

When I was in school back in the middle of the twentieth century, I learned that the ancients thought there were four elements that made up everything in the world — earth, air, water, and fire. Actually, I have since learned that Aristotle thought there was a fifth element — variously known as space, the void, the ether, non-matter, idea, and called by Aristotle quintessence. His reasoning went this way: All matter is subject to change, but the heavens do not appear to change. They are unchangeable, incorruptible; so they must be made of something different from the four earthly elements. Philosophers and scientists in other early cultures came to similar conclusions, and religions were built around this dualistic notion of a distinction between matter and non-matter — spirit, perhaps — that assigned values and supernatural personifications to each.

Each of the four earthly elements was tied to a cluster of other factors in life on earth—the senses, climatic conditions, the humours (which were thought to govern the condition of the human body). Water, for example, was related to taste and to coldness and, of course, wetness. Correspondingly, fire was hot and dry and governed sight, perhaps because it provided light. Earth was cold and dry and contributed to all the senses but particularly to touch and smell. Air was hot and wet and governed hearing. And it could probably be argued that the quintessence was responsible for thought and perhaps the soul or spirit.

Of course, now we know to a more or less limited extent what things are really made of, and we know that what is beyond the earth is neither unchangeable nor incorruptible. It is composed of the same elemental substances we encounter on earth. But is that all there is?

I think we can still learn something from this ancient view of the universe. We are inextricably related to these original four elements. We are grounded in earth. We are dependent on air and water for life and, in some ways, on fire as well—the physical fire that cooks our food and keeps us warm and lights our way at night and renews our world and the fire of passion that moves us in many ways for good or ill. And the quintessence? That can be the origin of ideas and aspirations, art and science, the sentience that is beyond the senses, and the relationships we may enjoy with the spirits of the universe, one or many.

So this little collection of work is organized around this old and nearly universal notion of the elements as I have experienced it. I hope you find in it something you can touch and taste, something that can warm and nourish you, a place you've been looking for, a music that gives you pleasure, a quintessence of the earth.

I wish to thank all the special people who have helped me along the way to this publication, but most particularly the members of my family who have served me as mentors and models for as long as I've been writing.

— *Rosemary Bergstrom*

Rocky Mountain National Park, Estes Park, Colorado

EARTH

LANDSCAPES

"Is Keith* still painting those funny little pictures of sky?" (Anon.)

Jacobshagen paints the plains
with an eye for the moment.
A faint whiff of fried chicken
on the mauve gray air,
the visible streak of blackbirds
harking in the distance,
the black thunder that billows
out of the southwest
are caught in the thin, dry washes
of oil on board
in his brief landscapes.

With my pen nearly dry
and my palette barely stained
with yellow cream and umber,
I try my hand at a geography —
an epiphanal poetics.
Like Jacobshagen,
I am after the quick artistry
of moments caught in
the amber of experience
like a fly out of time.
In the alchemy of
charcoal and azure evenings
is a beauty that is truth,
a perfect still life,
the where of what I am.

Now that landscape
washes up on brushy hills
and violet walls
and deeper, lower skies;
but still there's music
in the misty air.
Magpies, bluebirds, aspens
fade across the canvas,
but the same amalgam
of fresh earth and living
moments newly framed
and the same flag that waves
on a white front porch
in the near distance.

---

*"Keith" is Keith Jacobshagen, a well-known Nebraska artist famous for his small, intense, and highly evocative paintings of the Great Plains featuring remarkable skyscapes. The remark was made by a friend of his and reported by him during a presentation about his work at the University of Nebraska-Lincoln where he taught. It was often said of his work that it was so compelling that, in a picture of a farm, you could smell dinner cooking in the distant farmhouse, hear the thunderstorm moving in, and listen to the crows calling overhead — quite an accomplishment with just a little paint and canvas.

PLAINSWOMAN*

I saw her as I came down
the shallow incline into the cool interior,
glancing back over her shoulder,
startled, perhaps, at my approach.
She was young, but the plains
had already etched her face
with care and longing.
There was a gentle drift
to her deep green skirts
and her long dark hair,
as though the wind had been
strangely kind that day.

Romance was still there
in her eyes and in the folds
of her sleeve where it rested
on the wagon wheel, and
I wondered if her husband,
for surely she had one,
filled with worry for
the harvest and the stock,
knew that look or sought it there
and what it promised.

Her face was bronzed
by the lowering sun,
and there was a Virginian sort of arch
to her neck and her brow.
She touched her throat,
perhaps to loosen the collar
against the heat of the
summer afternoon.

She is cold and stiff now,
captured in molded metal
situated among the muted browns
creams and golds, rusty colors
that were her setting then
as they are now.
There are a few green trees
in the distance,
beyond the great windows
that frame her slender body,
but they do not seem
part of her natural landscape.

What can she have thought
of this land where all there was
to form a shadow was
what you brought with you
in the wagon or
dug from the sod?
And what would she think now,
her grandchildren long dead,
no crops at all in this place,
just the hot wind
and the crowded loneliness?

I'd like to think I know her
in this brief encounter,
but her eyes do not seek mine,
and I cannot read her soul there.
Our paths have only just crossed
in this quiet place
where she will alone remain
and I am the briefest visitor.

*In the Art Gallery of the Center for Great Plains Studies at the University of Nebraska-Lincoln, in an alcove walled by windows looking out on the campus there used to stand a lifesize bronze, startling in its realism, by Veryl Goodnight, called "No Turning Back." This piece is a response to that sculpture.

GARDEN

Here created,
a great feast for
all things wing-ed—
honeysuckle
for the hummers,
goldenrod for
autumn seekers—
butterfly bush
for the tiger
drifting on the
breezes blowing
herbal perfume
through the sun-warmed
summer languor—
water falling
from the rocks for
thirsty travelers
bathing among
ferns and lotus
'neath the branches
of the aspens—
wasps and dragons
sipping crystal—
coreopsis
tempting rabbits—
little brown birds
nibbling sedum—
chokecherries for
jays and robins—
planted for my
pleasure, giving
life to many
wanderers
in this
plentiful
sweet world.

LIVING ON THE PLAINS

Living on the plains,
with the blood red sun
setting in a sea
of forest ash
and the hot wind
blowing the life
out of every
still green thing
and energy
seeping away
like the last puddle
that was once a pond —
all that imagery
just lying around,
and I can't even
write a little poem.
Well, don't blame me.
What can you expect
now that the
Canadas are gone?

EARTH TO EARTH

I. PATRICK IS UNDER THE LILIES — A MEMORY

In the old days,
before AC,
we did the best we could
with what we had.
I sailed clothespin boats
in the stationary tubs
beside the wringer washer
in the dank basement.
Mom cooked whole meals there
on the old gas stove
left over from an earlier time.
We kept the shades lowered
and went about
in cotton underwear.
And after work
Dad took over
the red plastic wading pool.

Now, of course,
we move from
one conditioned space
to another
and eat salads
and drink gallons of
herbal sun tea.
And no one has
stationary tubs,
much less clothespins.
We're in control.

Still, when I wash
the tie-dyed shirts,
it seems to take
a long time in July
to rinse the detergent
from my cold fingers.
And when the heat is on,
Patrick,
who cannot bear
four walls for long,
is flat on his belly
under the lilies.

(Patrick was a 16-pound silver-tipped black part Maine Coon cat of very happy memory who died before his time.)

II. IN MEMORIAM
(to Macey)

There is still a hint of
golden silk and silver
on the rock and brushy
slope down to the water.
Deeply dreaming eyes yet
follow my steps to the
edge and, breathless, wait for
the arch of the stick high
through the clear morning air.

She was nurse and friend,
playmate and counsel
in the sad gray days
in a colder place,
trickster, child, wishing
star. We went our way,
we two, made our path,
found our new garden.

Memory is her home
now. She has slipped the lead
confining her to this
watery world, to my
fond embrace, and she runs
now ever in that bright
and bluer space where I
can still see her silvered
shadow in the night but
never touch that earth or
reach that land where she has
strayed so wild and free to
play forever the sweet
and carefree days away.

III. THE WALL

We built a wall
of smoke,
of bamboo,
of ignorance—
we built it high, then
we built it higher, so
high we could not see over;
so we climbed it, side by side.
When we reached the top and looked over,
we did not like what we saw, but by then
someone had been building the wall thicker and
stronger, filling the chinks with humanity and
fire and green things and orange and sounds and words
and fear; and the boundaries of the fear were the boundaries
of pain. So we climbed down and tried to dig under the wall,
to undermine its strength, and were nearly buried beneath the solid
illusion compacted of promises broken and repeated and
broken again. So we tore the wall down, stone by stone, word by word,
and we built a new wall, not to separate now but to bring
us together, not to hide behind but to work at.
We built it of granite, and on it we wrote the names
of the thousands whose lives paid its cost, the thousands
who ran into it and perished, the hundreds
who wrote the black story and set their mark
forever on its hardened face, the
hundreds who could not ignore it,
the scores who made it sacred,
the ones who live now only
in memory. And we promised
not to forget even
one who built
the first
wall.

Then we forgot.
For what false god
do we build
this new
wall.

IV. THE NEW GUARD

See them marching eight abreast
in their new pressed uniforms,
shiny medals on their chests,
draped each in colors,
four-hundred forty rows and growing
every day, marching
not to battle now
but coming home to stay.
These silent legions call us
to witness their return,
their entrance into memory,
and ten times their number
testify to the emptiness
of our allegiance to a covenant
we never meant to keep,
to the dismantling of a dream.
Where is the country we knew
when first we learned to sing
"America the Beautiful"?
Where are the children we were
who trusted the promising words?
Where are the flowers
among the whitened stones?

THE MYSTERY OF PEDAGOGY

I. CLASSROOM NOTES

Here you are with bright young faces
and new notebooks and those heavy
packs you carry, staring at me,
wondering who I am and what
I'll want from you. You cannot know
how scared I am beneath the mask
or what it costs for me to take
this place before you. You just come
and fill the seats from back to front.
You have that luxury.
                              I won't
ask you to open your books or
even to write things down today.
I've written it all down for you
today. But I have to speak it
so you will believe it, so you
will know it's true. And I have to
make you laugh at least once so we
can all breathe again, so we can
be less afraid of each other.

There's joy in all, a poet said.
There's joy in knowing I can teach you
something, joy in knowing you have
something I can learn from you 'tho
you do not yet know that you have
anything to teach. There's joy in
the enterprise we share, one with
another, making paths where there
was none before, stepping closer
to the present than we sometimes
dared before.

                        I want to tell you
how much joy you give me, but I
don't want to frighten you again
and see you scurry back to hide
behind the strange disguise you wear.
Joy brings responsibility,
and first you have to learn to take
the small burdens, the new little
ideas, before you lift this
heavier one.
                  But I know it.
It's why I'm here. It's why I know
I'll be here next week and next month.
It's why I can look at you now,
your bright shiny faces and your
new notebooks, and take off my mask.

II. HERDING CATS

Their faces are so clean,
like fresh washed slates.
They know all the answers,
but the questions are lost
in the eddies of emotion.
You can lead, but
will they follow? Or
will they slink off
like my aged cat who,
drunken on the catnip,
wanders an unthought of
path from sun to shadow,
surprised to find his way.
They, too, will make a path,
and we cannot chart it
for them. We can only
send them out with hope
to find their own sharp questions
and to build their own new world.

ON THE ROAD

      I

"In case of flood,
climb to safety."
Is there such a
place, I wonder.
Up the wall the
fire is waiting.
Down the canyon
water's rushing.
In the cave there
lurks the spirit
of another
time or journey
or the cougar's
evening hunger.
In the marble
halls the demons
leading astray
those who listen.
In the churches
are the shamans
telling penitential
stories
of the times no
one remembers,
shaking rattles,
charming vipers,
lighting candles,
sprinkling water.

Some are always
seeking safety,
climbing, buying,
begging, stealing,
any way they
think they'll find it.
But that way is
just illusion.

I think safety's
not illusion.
We find safety
by the river
on the path we
walk together,
fellow trav'llers
through the canyon,
walking in each
other's footsteps,
holding fast each
other's hand.

II
"Cows not mine."
It's a plaintive sign.
Is he feeling bereft
now the cows have all left
to find a new home?
Or was he always alone?
Or is he just annoyed
with everyone asking
if the cows on the road
are his? It's so taxing.
Or is it only the cows
that he's disowning
while the bull bides still,
his loving skills honing
against the day
when the cows come home,
to settle down
and no more roam.

Well, we'll never know.
That's the end of the poem.

AUTUMN JOURNEY

More than display of
bright scarlet leaves,
pale golden blooms
more than apple picking
late garden harvest
this season is known for
migration
west to east
north to south
high to low
animals heading home
to winter domiciles
as they have always done.

In August
Moraine Park was empty.
Only prairie dogs played there.
In September
big horns visit daily.
Herds of elk have come down
from the tundra
tending calves
bugling for new family.
Canadas fill the sky.

But no more hummingbirds.
They'll be back in spring.

MUSHROOMS AFTER RAIN

Between the green blades are
mushrooms after rain.
Just when it seemed
the dim remembered mist
would never part,
       here they are,
creamy white and succulent,
an enrichment
after barrenness,
an embarrassment
of riches,
well washed
and wished for
and never expected.

I gather them greedily,
preferring their pale chasteness,
dewy from the grass,
to ritual feasts.
I caress them
when I find them
springing from depressions
in an old landscape.
       They are mine.

This is a time for seeing
with rainy eyes
fresh treasures
beneath the aqua skies.

SEASONILLUSION

Such a warm night it was.
Yet the snow fell gently
in huge clusters
sometimes drifting sideways,
sometimes upward
toward the streetlight
and the laughing moon,
finally falling to ground,
gathering in eddies where
the pavement bent and broke,
filling in crevices
among rocks and thistles.
Jays, grackles, robins
all gone to nestling
in the nighttime quietude.

Then ... with one note, then another
the dawn chorus began
and the spell broken,
drifts of cottonwood seeds
lay everywhere about.

RECONCILIATION*

It's a painful lesson, friend:
Some things broken you can't mend.

The bird that can no longer fly,
the kite that's tangled far too high,
the threadbare clothes you've loved and worn,
the flower crushed, the branch that's torn,
the careless words that hurt the heart,
the empty space when lovers part,
the beaten child with pain too deep,
the promises you fail to keep,
the hunger that destroys the mind,
neglected ventures that unwind,
the wounds caused by a faithless friend,
the absence that will never end —
some things broken you can't mend.

Mental furniture outgrown,
daisy petals, snapped wishbone,
toys of childhood now unused,
songs of memory refused,
regret and guilt, a passion dead,
the fruitless quest, the thoughts unsaid,
the willing loss of innocence,
the dawning of experience —

painful lessons, but we bend.
Some things broken you don't mend.

*In a book called Necessary Losses, published in 1998, Judith Viorst teaches us that loss is a part of life and letting go is a part of growing up.

CHILDREN

I. GUARDIAN ANGELS

Where are those small fingers
caught in my hair, my clothes,
pulling me painfully
back to the perilous
now when I most need them?
Strange immortality
they gave me. Life was an
aching wonder at their
touch and in their bright eyes.
In darkened rooms I sought
them out, fragile in my
fear, and touched the silky
heads, the hand that reached in
sleep less dreamless than I
dared. No one is lost in
such a place of gentle
need. Now that I wander
tremulous and alone,
unguarded by those hands
of angels bending near with
care and tenderness, where
did the day go? Where is sleep?
Where are those fingertips
of light? How soon the night!

II. TOO MUCH IMAGINATION

Even a dimestore
turtle seemed out of
place in a small round
bowl. It needed a real
place to live, she thought.
So feeling sorry,
she built a brick wall
around a small patch
of weedy garden
behind the old house,
dug a shallow pond,
landscaped the space with
rocks, shells, and sand,
and brought the small green
turtle to its home.
By lunchtime it had
ventured three inches
toward the tiny pond.

Hours later and
after a shower,
the turtle was gone.
She searched the turtle
garden, then the yard,
then the neighborhood,
again and again
but with no success.
Where do turtles go
when it rains?

LEFT BEHIND

Shut the door.
Turn out the light.
No one's coming
here tonight.
Through the window
in the dark
lies a garden.
In the park
beyond the fence
no one ventures,
takes the chance
of a meeting
with a ghost.
But the ghost
sleeps in this room
beside me in the
bed we shared
when he was yet
the man he was
and I could still
remember how
the garden smelled
in sunlight.

A POST-MODERN GEOGRAPHY

Living as they do
on the painted surface of their lives,
as though the world
really were a plastic globe,
politically aligned,
full of largely empty spaces
painted blue,
they fail to guess
the lost dimension,
the depth their circle lacks,
the missed adventure.
Wine, like a river's flow,
defines their place,
not as wrinkles on a face
mark experience,
but more wanderingly,
dependent on each moment's
brief terrain.
Pain is strangely muted,
power an illusion,
decision scarcely possible,
joy displaced by fun,
love invariably brief,
reflection a mirror.
To probe, to sound
is to describe a radius
to a center one might reach
could one penetrate
beyond their prison
with its walls of air
and brittle pastel landscape
and too prominent bones.

Will their vision change?
Or will they ever wonder
at the strangeness of
the deep world's behavior
and, like a faithless soul,
retreat from its embrace.

LETTING GO

Behind the open door
that no one enters
I spin webs of kind
forgetfulness.
I can almost
believe now the
end will never come.
Rich harmonies
echo in this room.
I take up their strands
and play them through
the night deep with stars.
I can almost feel
a bright beginning
take shape in my hands
and slip gently
through these nervous
fingers. When I wake,
the blank light will have
washed the work away,
and I will be where
you can never find me.
Bind my head then and
take up the melody.
Something has broken
in our memory.

LEFTOVERS

Every holiday came
the same admonishment—
"Don't rip it. Be careful.
Let me have the paper."
And she would gently peel
tape, flatten the creases,
fold the gold, green, red, silver
wrappings, save the ribbons
from careless children,
playful cats. Into the
big brown box stored in the
hall closet it would go
with the tissue and tags,
safe for resurrection
to be used for the next
family festivity.

I found it there after
she herself was gone, the
carefully hoarded bows
and wrappings stored there for
holidays she'd never see
like the new slips and
nightgowns, the handkerchiefs
from Belgium and France, kept
for ceremonial
use, the scarves she never
wore, and letter paper
that would never see pen.
Perhaps she felt she did
not deserve the unworn
silky garments on her
aging, wrinkled flesh or
uncreased decorations
for her small charities.

Perhaps a lifetime of
thrift born of need in an
immigrant household where
nothing could be wasted
made a mortal sin of
discarding what could still
be used or soiling the
good linens or new clothes.
Or perhaps she simply
had never questioned the
customs of a culture
she inhabited but
never traveled or explored.

It's all gone now, gone but
not forgotten, treasured
in the attic of my
mind with memories of
careless children and the
dusty moments past and
yet to come when someone
searches through what I leave
behind when I am gone.

Cliffs above Watson Lake north of Fort Collins, Colorado

AIR

PASTORAL FANTASY*

I. ALLEGRO

Meadowlarks, blackbirds
piping, piping,
perched on the grasses,
sing to me, sing.
Sky over blue and
gold winter wheat
pictures flash by
my eyes in the music,
sharp and staccato,
fingers and talons.
Fly away. Ring through
wetland and field and
sing, sing, sing, sing.

II. ANDANTE

Now mid the waves of grasses
the stream meanders
feeding the rich earth
and her creations
a golden nectar,
a new breath of melody,
achingly sweet and filled with
the wandering spirit of
bright open spaces,
meeting the sky in
cerulean deep celebration,
echoing, echoing, echoing, echoing …

III. PRESTO AGITATO

There, the fox,
the fleet red fox
speeds through the
sunflowers,
bounding, intent
on the hunt,
and the rabbit,
still and then leaping,
flees at first here
and then there
and then back,
follows the verges,
tracks a new path.
This is a dance,
a jig through the wheat field.
Melody follows
the dances in whorls,
and changes and rhythms,
escaping at last
from the music,
a tableau in memory,
fantasy landscape,
the singer, the dancers
of a sudden ...
then gone!

A reflection on Fantasie Pastoral, a suite for oboe and piano by Eugene Bozza.

SALOME IN GRAY*

She will dance for you
in her drifting veils
of silk and silver.
She will lead you where
there is no path, this
graceful temptress with
scarlet roses and
starlight in her hair.
She will draw you through
the curtained doorway
where even night birds
and fox who haunt the
darkening wetland
will not follow,
gone now to their quiet
rest, to a place more
ancient than men's dreams,
to a shadow world
beyond memory.
First light reaches up
behind the gray hills.
Slowly she trails her
garments over land
barely colored in the
dim, chill new world
and with her bare feet
stirs the dew, weaves her
sinuous way through
the willows and the
stiff tall reeds — hardly
more substantial
than a whispered word.
And you will follow
straying far, ever
farther from your hearth
for the briefest chance
of an encounter.
Go then, piteous nomad;
chase the dream
across the empty plain.
Reach into the
beckoning red sky,
across the restless river.
Catch her if you can.
She will dance for you
there in the new day
just beyond your grasp.
But no, she will go,
lifting with the wind,
dancing on the dawn.

*The dance of the sandhill cranes on their stopover in central Nebraska is a compelling event for all lovers of wild birds.

ETCHING

Yesterday a chilling wind
from a place called "never summer"
blew away the misty scrim,
left the hills in sharp relief.
Each blade and stone and branch
became a study, India on vellum,
a crisply cut jet cameo
at the flushed throat of the canyon.
Now I see clearly the visage
washed clean of artifice
yet a finely styled picture
no mortal ever drew or dreamed.
There are images unseen,
unrecorded by a camera
or brush or pen that exist
only in the briefest glance
then in memory
or not at all,
places we visit just once
then never again.
Taste the moment.
Never let it pass you by
unremarked. No one
has ever inscribed it
just so.

The wind is gone now.
Mist obscures the mountains.
The white blanket
has been drawn up
over the peaks and valleys.
The half light of evening
gathers, glows, then goes.
Fade to black.

NIGHTCALL

My crystal breath
preceded me
down the dark road
beside the dam.
Tall grasses cracked
and whispered in
the night wind. Here
and there, yellow
oblongs of light
blinked on, blinked out.
I hurried my
steps toward the house,
then slowed, then stopped.
Far away and
high on the wind
the first call came.
A thin white line
traced a ragged
path against the
black moonless sky
and lifted me
out of time, 'til
high on the wind
I touched the home-
bound wanderers
and found the voice
to join the call,
to touch the earth.

SUNLIGHT

Ripples of light
play on the black bark,
reflections from
the half frozen pond.
The Canadas
are restless, hunting
in the dust for
the last bits of grain,
calling through the
naked trees, skidding
on the dark ice.
The chickadees and
finches at the
swaying goldenrod
flit nervously in
and out of vision.
Behind the glass
and lazy in the
melting sun, I
dream the ache away.
I think of you
on the road again,
your silence deep
in my mind where the
sunlight cannot
reach. The birds and the
flickering pond,
the whispering grass
between ancient rocks
cannot bring you back.
I dream you in
the silvering sun.

NEW YEAR

When the last dry leaves
have slipped the trees
and silent falls the snow,

on a windless day
in the dying year,
join hands with me and go

where music rings
in the cold clear air
and, deeper than our dreams,

we feel the first
faint stirrings of
a new year's freshening streams.

Then speak a word
of blessing on
a faded world made new.

Recall the promise
of new life, and
peace will be in you.

EPHEMERA

Experience —
like a first snow —
comes unlooked for
to a world still
green and growing,
though with a hint
of gold and crimson,
each day melting
into consciousness,
each single moment
sharp or faded,
wrapped in emotion,
whispering, drifting,
within or beyond
our reach, is shaped
into memory,
frozen there — or gone.

THE MORNING WIND

That early summer
camped on the side of
Harney Peak in the
still sacred Black Hills
above Sylvan Lake,
the snow still nibbling
at the black moss rocks,
it was cold in the
tent, too early in
the year, and we were
unprepared for the
conditions. All day
and all night the wind
rushed and sang among
the pines, a voice of
the earth we could not
forget. Stay with us
a moment at the
edge of a new day.
Listen to the wind
whispering, calling
now to you from the
shadowed mountaintop.
Look up to the black
sky, so full of stars,
and touch the earth, the
warm gentle mother.
And know there is a
world that is at peace.

ECONOMY

Empty, ready
for your family;
multi-story
open floor plan;
solid building.
Lots of room for
children to play.
Wonderful view;
open spaces;
close to food stores.
Reduced for quick
occupancy,
offers welcome.

They considered
all their options.
The construction
was surely sound.
Great location.
Okay, he said.
The pair moved in.

Driving past on
my way to shop,
I spotted them,
looking settled
in the window
of the silo,
long abandoned
in the bare field,
the pair of great-
horned owls, watchful,
basking in the
morning sunshine,
contemplating
the coming eggs.
Just another
family planning.

RAPTOR

Small grey
brown and white
feathers scattered
across the green —
a visitor
at dawn perhaps
an early meal
for a great-winged
sailor of the wind
and nothing left —
but these remnants
a reminder.

EREMITE

In your mountain aerie
you feel safe, untouched
by worldly waywardness,
wrapped in the music
of ten thousand pines,
breathing the thin
untainted air, removed
from fretful contact.

But the demons will find you
even here, rub the raw
places in your pale soul.
You call them when they
stray too far abroad.
And there is the dread
of the precipitous
descent into that land
where waters lie stagnant
and the earth is flat and gray.
You would as soon pull up
the soft white blanket
and sleep the moons away,
safe from a human touch,
alone beneath the sky,
so cold and pure and dead.

CHANSONS POUR LES OISEAUX (SONGS FOR THE BIRDS)

I. DAWN

The moon has slipped beyond the hills,
leaving a thin silver film of silk
against the blue black sky
above the marsh. Catkins are soldiering
through the still water, only a faint
riffle to shadow her passing.
She has left a few glittering sentinels
to keep watch for day.
But here and there the voices have begun,
clear, sharp notes and gentle chittering.
They speak to one another and to me
as I watch with them the
mellowing eastern sky for the approach
of another light, unborrowed and
alone above the no more silent willows,
green waters filled with life and sound,
the voices swelling and choralling
on the bright golden scented air.

II. BLACKBIRDS

The blackbirds come every day.
They don't mind the deep drifts
or the greedy rock doves
crowding over the ungleaned seeds.
I hear them call in fluted notes and
see the flashing gold and scarlet
chevrons of their wings
echoing the summer roses
newly wrapped in frost.

III. COLLAGE

The pelicans and egrets have returned,
their bright white raiment
stark against the turquoise pond,
and summer's at the flood.
They strut and preen
at edges of this world
and watch with sharpened sight
the smallest movement
on the cattail patterned silk.
Sandpipers nibble at the verge,
and hummers in the juniper about
sing nectarous songs.
Everywhere the children
flap and feed upon their elders,
shored among the pink and yellow
marsh mallow and sweet clover blooms.
And wild white roses echo on the green.

IV. NIGHTFALL

A rush of dusky blue
settles to the marsh.
Eyes still sharp for careless creatures
caught among the reeds,
she steps with careful grace
across the gently rippling pools
afire with molten gold and amethyst,
crowned with flame,
while high above the nighthawk calls
the creatures shy of day to venture here,
begin the celebration.
Life sustains in silent jubilation.
Wings confer a gentle benediction.

V. ARGUMENT

The stellar jays are quarrelling over
who will have the picnic
bread and cheese, first one
and then another chain of
irascible chatter, their
prussian blue jackets and
spiked black helmets darting
here and there in the summer sun,
disputing the possession,
while opportunistic magpies
steal the feast.

VI. LAMENT

There he lies fallen
on the brackish weeds,
his teal and chestnut garment
dulled now by the sucking mud,
his voice of quiet comfort now unheard.
She in faithfulness beside
calls plaintively but cannot raise
the breath so stilled.
Just a bird, you say,
but all earth's creatures mourn
the chilling end of day.

VII. HOMECOMING

Distant lines writ high and largely
silent on the azure wind—
Then clear across still water
the first faint notes of coming home.
The gatherers are returning from the fields
to taste the tangy liquid stream,
to nurture and to breathe familiar air.
Their well worn quaker garments,
stiff white collars, sharpening voices
fill the weedy world.
Sweet grasses, milkweed, thistle
send up welcome as they
skim the surface, settle in,
and glide in gathering crowds
of witness to the splendor
of this deepening wilderdream.

This collection of seven poems was inspired by a suite of seven miniatures composed for solo oboe by the late British musician and composer Paul Reade. The Reade work is called "Aspects of a Landscape" and consists of the following movements: Dawn, Birdsong, Bird-Movements, Sun Dance, Conflicts, Lament, and Celebration. The oboe suite with the accompanying poems was first presented at a "Music in the Mountains" concert at Rocky Ridge Music Camp in Allenspark, Colorado, and subsequently at the 37th Annual International Double Reed Convention in Provo, Utah, in July 2008. The performers at both of these venues were William McMullen (oboe) and Charles "Chip" Smith (baritone).

SMOKE

I sat in the brown chair,
like a dry old womb.
You sat on the bed
made of mattresses
stacked on the floor.
Late afternoon filled the room,
and the scent of incense
curled among the shafts of sun.
We lit cigarettes,
watched the silver clouds
rise and encircle
the blue rings of musk,
play in patterns
like a visible melody
on the rose watered silk light.
We listened to
its fragile cadences.

There is nothing profound
in shared silences
or in smoke.
There is only
a simple poetry,
moments stripped
to the essential.
There is only
a necessary
relationship
transcending time.

WINGDOM

Up the ladder of geese
to a vantage point above
the maze of lakes and fields
I go where I can see
roads circling 'round farmsteads,
fences defining human conditions
of living. Yet the tracks
follow no such pattern; they are
random across the snowy plain.
The kestrel, harrier, redtail
strike where they choose from wire,
cottonwood, power pole;
and in the meandering ditch
a gang of dippers pursue their
daily business unassailed.
Reigning over all, uncaring
for the road or fence or
farmers' quaint arrangements
the eagle watches for the weaknesses
in lake ice and in flock,
keeps court in that uncertain domain
of watcher and watched—
Oh icon, what are gates and
fences to this great governor
of air and untouched landscape.
Returned to earthly trail and hedge,
I celebrate this pastoral sovereignty.

Cache le Poudre River, north central Colorado

WATER

LIKE WATER

Water finds a way
or makes one.
Winter is no bar.
There beneath the ice
where fish dream
she drifts or courses.
Nor rock can stay
the slow but steady
blade she wields
refashioning the earth.
Down canyon walls
she trickles, washes
for a day, a season,
always seeking
where she might find rest.
But nowhere can she
end. And in the mind
the thought, like water,
seeks its path,
uncharted and unruled,
where it will, sharp-edged,
makes its way
through densities,
building to a
river through the canyon
it has shaped
and, like the water,
wanders with no rest,
an endless re-creation.

THE THING WITH FEATHERS

What is common to
all creation is
movement, difference —
that we make, that we
witness or suffer,
that we conceive of,
that we may become.

In the season of
resolution, change
is everywhere. See,
the days grow longer,
the creatures stir and
begin to wake. The
whisper of coming
miracles breaks the
winter's deep silence.

Let it be a dance,
this new and always
renewing life's breath.
Let it be a song
of peace, reunion
with the bright angels
of another time.
Let it be for us
a promise that is
finally fulfilled.

SHAPE SHIFTING

I. MORNING FOG

In an hour
the sun will
turn off the
mist that creeps
into the
garden from
across the
silent lake.
The morning
birds will fly,
the dew dry
off the leaves.
Then it will
be too late
to speak of
hidden things.

But for now
while time is
caught in this
silent mist
and the webs
are strung with
pearls in the
twisted trees,
I may dare
contemplate
dangerous
reflections
in the glass,
those moments
of the mind
free of the
commonplace
relations,
those moments
seen through the
cracks in the
closed door of
memory,
visible
heat in the
scented air,
pleasure and
pain in the
unlooked for
encounter,
touching the
earth, watchful
in veils of
amethyst
shadows — Then
it is day.
The moment
is gone now,
gone in the
killing sun.

II. FROST

Those few moments
bathed in crystal
at the apex
of the morning
slip into
consciousness
with the sudden
clarity of
fire flowers.
They are rapture
but no more
eternal
than a word
escaped beyond
understanding,
touched by careless
sunlight and a
memory.
What we may keep
unfading is
ephemeral,
like the hint of
first light, lost in
merciless noon.

III. TRAPPED

On a still night,
the air thick with
locusts' harping
and the hot breath
of anticipation,
I looked into
the watery glass
and saw only a
reflected passion.
The year has reached
dead calm, and all
the yearning that
I felt in spring
has turned to lead
congealing in
the cauldron.
What if morning
never comes, and
I stand staring in
the empty glass
until time ends.

LETTER TO SYLVIA*

When you had cast off the
last ropes and your small craft
drifted away from the
shore, when you no longer
heard the voices of the
angels crying and the
world had lost all color
in the gray rain, when you
cut the rings from your cold
fingers and locked the door
against the last friend, when
you laid your weary head
on the hard floor and breathed
the sweet smoke, did your eyes
burn with the crystalline
vision of your last poems?
Did you see then where we
cannot? Did you learn the
secret no one else can
tell us and you never
now can share? Did you find
a home at last? Or will
you be a wanderer
forever from the chill
north city of despair.
I am listening — but
I can't hear the answers.

*Sylvia Plath was a brilliant and distinguished American poet, wife of British poet Ted Hughes, mother of two, who after years of depression committed suicide by inhaling carbon monoxide gas from the oven in her apartment. She was just 31 years of age, separated from her husband at the time, and her children were asleep in an adjoining room of the flat.

WHERE I LIVE

I don't live here.
Cold, brittle, dry, and flat
never was my country.
When I look out my
innermost window,
I see a sky
amber and liquid
above a green sea.
I hear the boom
and crash of waves forming
and reforming
washed up from a place
I'll never know.
Dolphins play and feast
beyond the breakers.
The air is filled with salt
and white dune roses,
and the laughing gulls
and ghost crabs
call me home.
When I am afraid,
I remember where I live
and breathe again.

DREAM WHORLS
(for Helen, Kate, Joyce, Fran, Betty, Judy ...)

Where it began you can't say,
this familiar path down to
the water. It must have been
meeting old friends at that
wedding, seeing a cousin,
the long walk down the hall
at the hotel conference.
But these things don't just happen,
do they? You're twenty-three,
but even youth won't take you
stepwise from Laguna Beach
to Lake Michigan's flat sands
where now you trace
not the old aristocracy
of summer memory
in middle years but some
odd reflection deeper
into streets you knew in childhood.
How did you come here?
to meet these people vanished
so long from your world?
In this impossibly
recreated landscape
of strange and unstrange shores?
And to what purpose at
this gathering age when
no wounds can be healed and
the tide is running out?
But as you see these faces
and step spirals in the sand,
this, finally, is a
question you can answer.

COQUINA BEACH
Hatteras Island, North Carolina, early summer ...

There is a place so strange
it must be illusion —
where the soft pink air
meets the silver green sea
and the pale gold sand and
they become one element,
indistinguishable,
no boundaries, no time.
The easterly vista
is a reflection of
the west, joined to it
by only a fingernail
of dune and wind-blown sea oats.
On the wide flat empty beach,
cleaned of shells and driftwood
by the relentless tides
and the gray nor'easter
and the lone gatherers,
there are only the scurrying
ghost crabs and cloud shadows,
fairy terns darting above
the water and the rays'
egg cases washing up
to draw the eye from the
fading horizon. And
you can walk forever
down the imperceptible
slope into the water
lapping gently at the sand.
You only become one
more color in the
unchanging panorama.
And you would miss
the tiny white triangles
of coquina shells unless
you sunk down to the warm sand
and searched them out.

Too soon the day is ending.
The osprey returns to the nest.
The rosy sky deepens,
and the silent watchers
descend to the sand and
stand with folded white wings,
their eyes lifted to the
glowing west, their backs turned
to the violet water
and the dolphins far beyond
the fading shoals to witness
to the end of day. You turn
your steps toward the old
gray unpainted cottage
and leave the mysteries
to the night and its creatures.

There are places where the
wandering spirit can
take its rest and know
other spirits still watch
and protect and refresh
and transform the dark world
to something sacred,
something mystical.
It is salvation
to find such a place,
to recognize what it is,
and to carry it with you
wherever you go.

CANYONS

There are mysteries in the canyons,
eyes that watch in silence for
life and purpose beneath the spruce
among the whispering grasses.
Careless footsteps find no path there.
Shadows play beneath the water
of the swift stream, the spill of glaciers
between the rusty walls
to plains, to other rivers,
other lands with no place to hide.
This is a place of secrets,
of hidden moments and profound
perception, of meditation,
of reverence and
sweet release.

ROARING RIVER

Rushing from a cleft in the mountain,
spilled from some unseen lake
above a lake above a lake
high on the brooding granite face,
she filled the sleeping valley,
spread life among the vetiver,
refreshed the summer elk and coyote.
But now the icy breath
that howls through the bare aspens
stops her in her path through
the white washed world.
No more glittering in bright sun,
she is dusty slate at my feet.
Nibbling at smooth rocks,
she seals the mysteries
of her deeper pools
with bands of steel and silver.
Yet beneath restraint,
her voice cannot be silenced.
She goes on telling,
telling stories filled with promise,
speaking truth to mountains.
Who hears? Who answers?

BIG THOMPSON

The centuries go by the window
in jagged procession,
thrust upward by some
seismic shudder
in the nearly distant past.
The horizon approaches
with relentless force,
meets the moment and engulfs it.
Furious waters rush down,
devour the rock in their path,
leave shards of memory behind.
There is nothing gentle here,
though warm sun washes everything
and flowers, gold and purple,
cling to cliffs and braes,
home to scissored swallows,
sharp featured hawks.
The trees survive in hollows
or bravely lodged in clefts
of canyon walls or
clustered near the tumbling water.
Bighorns surely venture
down the face to reach
the grassy verge, the swords of mullein.
We are strangers here,
rude interlopers in a forbidden place,
permitted just a moment
to intrude and then move on,
lessons yet unlearned.

WATERS

Just five words
at the end of a story
but they hung in my mind
long into my life.
They were my story too—
"haunted by waters."

A Great Lake
bounded my childhood,
sunny beaches, long friends
are all submerged
in that green blue memory.

Many rivers run through it—
the Chicago, running backward
through the city of my birth;
the Platte, shallow and flat,
springtime home to
many million geese, ducks,
half a million cranes, waiting eagles;
the Poudre and Thompson,
slicing through rock, building canyons,
sending out richness
to nourish land, wildlife.

Grandest of all, mighty Atlantic,
you were my deepest classroom,
teaching me letter by letter—
Avon to laughing gull to mahi mahi,
nor-easter to Okracoke to whale.

So much part of my life,
the closeness, essence, beauty
of water, yet I am not
nor ever have been
a creature of water.
That too is part of the sad story,
part of the haunting.

REDWING MARSH

Broad gray-blue wings circled
in a narrowing arc
over the pea-green pond,
golden eyes searching for
the one perfect cove
rich with silver fish,
then descending gently,
surveying the aquascape,
grooming after flight,
celebrating a new home.

The Canada families
sail by, greetings exchanged
with a new neighbor.
Mallards must be told, of course,
but they're mostly absent.
Reedy fringes are
peacefully singing.

Then …
Out of the north come
two more great blue pairs of wings
circling the first
who rises to meet them
but not to greet them,
rather to claim what is his.

Now the peace is over.
Singers rise to challenge,
small black tenors,
red chevrons on their wings:
"Surely you can read the signs.
This is Redwing Marsh.
There is no bluewing landing here.
Be off. Be off. And come no more
to threaten our tranquility."
And in a rush of
crimson, gold and black,
the big blue wings are beaten back.

Quietude's returned—
Gentle rain, two sandpipers—
Stillness without wings.

Sunset over Mesa Verde, Colorado

FIRE

THE FIRE OF PASSION

I. DANCERS

It begins
        tentatively
like the bolero
slow
and a little uncertain
you turn,
        he turns
you circle each other
        in narrowing arcs
reaching out of need
        to touch and
        be touched
        and you do
and feeling floods you
        deeper than
        familiar channels
you step back
but are drawn
into the flowing
        more tightly circling
        circling music
beating so deep in
        your body
you feel its echoing
heat in your mind,
        your soul,
        your senses reeling ...
and the dance may go
        on and on
or end.

II. DIMENSIONS

Tonight I met a ghost.
My hand, wraithlike, reached
out toward his fingers.
No one saw the movement.
No one saw the tears
gather in corners
and fall silently
into the heavy
emptiness between
our searching eyes.
He came from a far
away world I thought
was dead, buried in
the chaos of my
ordinary life.
He came in darkness,
drawing me into
the quiet circle
of his world, waking
the words I never
spoke in that distant
land of memory
and white heat. When I
turned away, the door
had closed forever
on the present,
imprisoning me
in molten glass where
the hand moves ever
closer but never
do the fingers touch,
the eyes drop crystal
rain which will never reach
the earth, the heart speaks
in whispers passions
no one ever hears.

III. THE LOVER: A VILLANELLE

My heart remembers every word you say,
Though few and far between the words may be;
Each time we meet, you take my breath away.

Only my eyes say what I cannot say
when from across the room you smile at me.
My heart remembers every word you say.

There is no future; there is just today.
There is no crowded room — just you, just me.
Each time we meet, you take my breath away.

You steal my dreams. I'm lost in endless day,
but night would bring me no serenity.
My heart remembers every word you say.

There is no charm, nothing I do or say,
No hope that you will ever set me free.
Each time we meet, you take my breath away.

It's many years since you last smiled at me,
years you were gone. Did you once think of me?
My heart remembers every word you say.
Each time we meet, you take my breath away.

IV. OBSESSION

You wander through my dreams
like a phantom, but I
know each line in your hand
like I know my own landscape.
Your heart beats in me,
keeping time in my mind,
with my heart, beating sure
as the clock in the tower,
rhythmic and deep as the sea.
You linger on my
senses like an unnamed
perfume caught in the wake
of a stranger passing.
I can no more silence
your persistent telling
of lives I think you led
than I can my own thoughts.
You are the world I dream
but inhabit, the burden
I take up each morning,
the journey I can't break
at evening, the refuge
I take from the empty
and silent afternoon.
I am alone with you.
And should I wake from my
dark dream, I wake into
unending day where you
only live, breathe, retell,
continue the story,
a guide without substance
to nowhere I can go,
to no one who touches
me, only returning
to you, to you, to you.

V. ESSE MACHINA AMORATA

When is love wrong?
    What makes it so?
        Is it the object
of love or the lover
    who determines
        that direction?
And is that direction
    merely physical
        or moral in nature?
Is love in fact
    ever truly wrong
        if honestly engaged?

This complex machine —
    for we are all that,
        made by man or born —
loves that equally
    complex machine
        judged by someone
not to be someone
    to be touched, entered,
        loved in the deepest sense
because of a
    barrier built
        of natural laws,
laws made by human machines.
    Where then is the
        obligation?
How do they determine
    their ultimate fate?
        Love should always matter
more than someone's law.

And we're back to
    the beginning,
        the center of
the labyrinth.

THE POETICS OF FIRE

I. FIRE

Everything I write now
becomes correspondence,
a recital of longing to live,
failing to sing new songs,
speaking your name in the
deep blue emptiness of smoke,
filling the page with words
I can never send
across bleak and silent
windy miles. Now
when I need you
in the night, you have
abandoned the labyrinth
while I still search
and struggle at the center.
Teach me again the
words of your song.
Sing me awake with your
fiery voice. Fold me now
into your life. Let me sing
you to sleep tonight.

II. BROKEN DIALOG

    You listen to
    me with your mouth
    choosing the words
    it seems to you
        I ought to say
    and waiting for
    your turn to speak.
I listen to
        you with my eyes
and hear only
what you try not
    ever to tell.
        I am waiting
        for the first real
        conversation
        we may someday have.

III. DISPARATE POETS

You are so
sure of tongue.
And I lisp
quietly
along in
your neat wake.
Where do the
lines cross? Where
are the right
words hiding?
And what can
we have to
say to one
another
when you look
always in
and I look
beyond the
horizon?

IV. WRITING POETRY

    I drag each word
       screaming into
the light of day
    and tuck them in
neatly around
    the frayed edges
    of my broken
thoughts. They have a
    life of their own
    and will not stay
where I put them
but rearrange
    themselves in time
to a music
I never heard
    when I sounded
    them out of their
hiding places.
So what they make
    is not what I
had in mind but
    something truer.

V. COFFEEHOUSE CASUALTIES

In this place
reeking of
rich warm brews
and burned out
cigarettes,
oils and pots
and notebooks,
sometimes
lives touch, raw
ends exposed.
You have to
be ready
for the pain.
It always
comes, rubbing
on the soft
edges of
your mind.
And you can't
give it back.

THE POLITICS OF FIRE

I. CONUNDRUM

They told me,
"Don't tear that flag,
 it's a sin against the country!"
Then they forgot my soldier son,
 his blood spilled in foreign sand,
 and they soiled my deep blue skies
 and blotted out the stars.

They told me,
"Keep that white house white;
 it was never meant for colors!"
Then they papered it
 in green and red
 and offered it for sale.

They told me,
"Sing that anthem proud,
 make it ring around the world!"
But the machines and lies and hate
 were just too loud,
 too loud and 'reft of music.

They told me to
"recite the pledge,
 the promise to my country!"
Then they took away
 my liberty.
They beat back
 my equality.
They broke
 the founders' promises.
They scattered
 justice, mercy, peace
 like dust upon a grave.

So who am I?
And where am I?
And what do I do now
 when there is no one left
 I trust to tell me?

In The Echo Maker *(2006), Richard Powers has one of his characters, a psychologist, ask what it is about the human species that makes it "save the symbol" and discard the thing it stands for.*

II. STREET SCENE
Paris, 2015

Sitting in their chairs
before the café
watching life go by
on the avenue
sipping their sweet drinks
exchanging a word
now and again

then

suddenly it is chaos
a man appears
a gun is raised
out of nowhere
deliberately
first one falls
then another
then the third
three are dead
on the pavement
the gun is lowered
the dark figure
slow calm
without care
steps away
from the scene
like an actor
leaves a set
with no emotion

curtain

III. TERROR BY OTHER NAMES

Terrorism—
It's in the news
or on the streets.
We'd know it if
we met with it.
It wears a hood
and speaks language
not like our own.
It uses bombs
and foreign guns.
It comes from where
they speak of god
in other tongues.

But is that true?

Here in our town
a child lies dead
by her own hand,
terrorized by
her own classmates
so we have heard
for some difference
they chose for a
target without
shame or purpose.
It was their own
private jihad—
brief, domestic,
just as deadly.

IV. COMMON DENOMINATOR

Hamas fires rockets into Israeli settlements.
Israeli children wounded, killed.
Israel fires rockets into Gaza.
Palestinian children wounded, killed.
Israel blames Hamas for
placing rockets in settlements.
Hamas blames Israel for
targeting settlements.
US Congress vows to fight drug cartels
to protect our children.
US Congress seeks to deny asylum
to refugee Central American children
fleeing drug cartels.
Twenty-one-year-old American mother of five
beats infant daughter to death.
Texts boyfriend next morning,
"I must have been pretty drunk last night."

V. ANTHEM

For all the beaten women,
The children terrorized,
The victims who did not survive,
The broken bleeding lives—
We're here to tell their story,
To fight for what is right.
For them we raise our voices.
We will take back the night.

We live our lives imprisoned,
Confined by our own fear.
We cannot walk alone at night.
We know the threat is near.
We owe it to our daughters
To educate our men.
To teach them is to free them
So no one's hurt again.

We stand together, sisters
And brothers in the fight.
Together we are stronger
To fight for what is right.
Together every color—
Black, red, yellow, brown, and white—
We sing our bright new anthem:
We will take back the night.

THE WARMTH OF FIRE

I. THE LETTER

Lollipops and mistletoe and candy canes,
Stockings filled with toys and dreams and old refrains—
Christmas eve, and home is where
My heart will always be.
I'll miss you all this Christmas.
Light a candle there for me.

Ornaments and colored lights and silver bells,
Carolers outside your door, the sweet noels,
Sugar cookies, Christmas cards
From near and distant friends—
I'll miss them all this Christmas
And the presents Santa sends.

I would build a snowman.
You would trim the tree,
Tell the Christmas story,
Share the holiday with me.

Here's my Christmas wish list for us next year:
Christmas morning I'll be there with you, my dear.
The sweet old music echoing,
The warmth of fire's glow—
I'll be with you next Christmas
To watch the falling snow.

I read the letter every year about this time.
A glass of wine, a candle shines, it's Christmastime.
The silver bells are ringing and
The carolers still sing,
But I miss you most at Christmas,
And I'll always wear your ring.

II. HOME FOR CHRISTMAS

The colored lights
caught in gently
turning glass frame
the image like
an old-time movie.
Time is frozen
in the tinseled
memories and
hangs in the stale air.
Just two weeks since
I sat in this
same chair waiting
for you to come home.
I had waited
two long months then.
Tonight I am
waiting again,
trying not to
remember that
you came and are
gone again, back
to your separate life.
Candles flicker
and the bits of
colored glass turn
slowly, catching
fire from faerie lights,
memories hung
branch by branch in
forms that do not fade.
And the moment
of my waiting
is frozen in
the moment of
my emptiness
and turns slowly,
slowly in the
dancing gold light.

Fossil Creek Reservior Regional Open Space, Fort Collins, Colorado

QUINTESSENCE

RAINBOW

In that brief space
between darkness
and daylight when
the sky wears a
rainbow cape from
violet zenith to
scarlet horizon,
she welcomes him
returning from the
uncreated world
she cannot know.
The mists recede
at his approach
from the rivers
and low places.
Only the brightest
travelers among
the stars still sing
about her, a
silent cantata.
In that still interval,
that glorious caesura
of a chill morning
is forged a new
covenant among
the elements.
Imagination
is epiphanal.
Peace is a thing
you can hold in your hand.
The eternal is
captive of the
of the moment.
And then the moment
is gone.

TARANTULA*

Ever faster she spins,
and the tightening circles
draw in, surround, entrap
the objects of her strange
and empty desire
where they struggle vainly,
unable to withdraw,
unwilling to cut the silk
threads of her prison,
bewitched by her cold lust.

And she, dizzy and pale
from the mad dance,
drunk with the passions
she dares not admit
to consciousness,
stands alone amid the chaos
that is her one
dark act of creation.

*Tarantula: [from Taranto, Italy], a European wolf spider (Lycosa tarentula) popularly held to be the cause of tarantism, a form of madness.

CELESTIAL ENCOUNTERS

I. JOURNEY
(Appleton WI to Lincoln NE, January 1989)

I traveled east to west,
chasing the fleeing deer
'til it plunged headlong
below the horizon,
pursued by the spreading glow
of the reddening vault at my back.
Overtaken at last by noon,
I followed the sun in its fall
to a deepening sea of red;
and glancing once over my shoulder,
I beheld — oh wonderful symmetry —
the deer with her silvering flanks,
just mounting the indigo night.

II. FULL MOON
*(Pioneer Boulevard, Lincoln NE,
January 1980)*

We nearly met last night.
You upon the farther hill,
I the nearer stood,
a moment only, 'til
my thoughtless movement
took me from your sight.
You were constant. It was
I who disappeared.
Yet the memory of
your full radiant form
just lingering on that crest
will shadow all my world
in nights unspent.

III. NEW MOON
*(Van Dorn Avenue, Lincoln NE,
Christmas 1979)*

There at the crest of
the hill, suddenly
the new moon rises
from her earthen bed.
"There is more to me
than most folk see,"
said the moon
in her silver voice,
"and I think
there is more to you."
"And does that matter?"
She responded,
"No matter, if there is spirit …"
And her voice came back
from farther still until
the music of her laughter
was lost among the stars.

BROKEN MIRROR

Remember? ... sure, I remember ...
All of us of an age in the day
remember ... where we were, how we heard,
what we did. I was just hanging out
in the college newsroom, playing cards.
Then the door opened — to silence —
where there should have been laughter,
people coming, going, eating lunch,
greeting friends, sharing notes — just silence.
Someone came in then and said,
"The president is dead."
What were we doing there,
preparing for a future that
would never come, that gray November.

Remember? ... yeah, I remember ...
the sunny September morning ...
then the phone rang: "Turn on the TV."
And there it was, smoking tower,
second plane, fire exploding
into clear blue sky,
bodies falling, falling to earth,
steel, concrete, sky itself falling,
falling through dense gray air,
falling forever, filling our lives
with black apprehension,
fear of a future we did not
conceive, born of a spell of some
other's conjuring in that endless
blue gray September morning.

Remember? ... oh, yes, I remember ...
It's the moment that creates
the future. We wait for something
we know is coming, and something
unimagined suddenly is there
in the space that once was fall morning,
November afternoon, Friday evening
before Easter or school day noon.
And you are nowhere you have ever been,
but there is nowhere else to go,
no place you know, and all around
the sky is falling down.
O strange new world
that has such monsters in it!

IMMANENCE

Where do we find the eternal, the sacred encounter?
I have felt it in a whale's warm wet breath on my face —
in half a million sandhill cranes lifting off the Platte
in the red dawn, singing to the sun —
in the sound of rushing water beneath the silver ice —
in the bugling of elk in the golden autumn distance —
in the midnight call of coyotes
and the evening lines of geese above my roof —
in the eagle in the cottonwood next door
and the prairie falcon hunting in my garden —
in the whisper of wind in perfumed trees on the Pine Ridge —
in the clear silent lake set like a jewel in a ring of mountains —
in the boom and tang of the surf transformed
to the gentle lap of the encroaching tide
on the wide flat star-strewn beach —
in my grandmother's eyes and my granddaughter's laugh.

I cannot tell you how it is
the wind is my angel
playing in the lilacs and
the deep clear blue above.
I can't explain why
the water speaks to me now
as it never has to you
or what atom of creation
lives in its crystal deeps.
I've never known why my voice responds
to the soloing red bird
or where it learned to speak
in the red tail's tongue.
The language of the melting snow
is just as clear to me
as my child's speech,
but how that came to be is mystery.

I don't believe we ever left the garden.
I think we lost the art of embracing the encounter.
We still live in Eden. We just need
to open our human hearts
to its transcendent presence
to share in its abundance.

TIME

Time is no constant.
Feel the slow creep of
minutes as you wait
for the gift of each
cool new morning or
the evening's heated
passion. See the days,
hours, years canter by
like eight beautiful
blue horses, one life,
brief or long though it
may be, fading in
the dim distance, one
arcing gracefully
into beginning.

They say time is a
river we never
step in twice and know
it is the same. Yes,
that may be so, but
in a river two
souls can visit the
same water, one who
stands above the falls
and one below, each
within the other's
sight, and time and place
will shift and change as
they partake of the
same reality.
And if one joins the
other above or
below, how do we
measure time for one,
the other, or the
relentless fall of
the stream of water.
Time is no constant,
and the river will
never reach an end.

REFLECTIONS

In that midnight
just beyond the
sanctuary
on Christmas eve
where snow lingers
on the dry grass
are thousands of
stars among the
branches of the
spruce and elm trees,
a flickering
reflection of
the Christmas trees
within and of
so many years
and other trees
and stars, yet still
more real, this framed
illusion, than
the insubstantial
space I occupy.
Where have all those
celebrations
fled, and am I
there now or just
part of the dark
reflection? Where
did the happy
new years go! And
will there ever
be another?
Then the chimes rang.
The gathered crowd
stood and sang a
simple carol,
greeted neighbors,
said their credos.

And in the dark
all at once there
came an answer.
It was always
in the warmth and
comfort of the
sanctuary.
Be of good cheer.
The heart and mind
have always been
great enough to
contemplate the
reflection and
reality.
The past is there
in memory.
The future is
unreachable.
The present is
a gift to all
the celebrants.
Be not afraid.
Choose the morning.
Dare go forward.

PERSPECTIVE

It was a beautiful
September morning.
It's what they always say,
just like today — sky so blue.
That's what they say.
So it must be true.
Once there were two towers there
standing bold and tall
reaching toward the sky
in the early autumn sunlight
and then a flash
and then eruption
and then so many die.

On that clean blue screen
that is our memory,
we will always see
two towers in the morning sun,
two silver planes, two arrows,
first one, splitting the smart face,
releasing the fire, the ash,
then the other, cutting through the steel,
the glass, the sand and dust,
creating a different candle in the sun,
a strange moment of fantasy
within a fast-rising sea of reality.

What did you think, mother,
when you heard your son speak to you
out of eternity
riding that shining missile
into our deep dark memory,
forever with us now,
one of our own.
Who is he now, mother?
Who are you?

September morning,
gold and blue —
it's what they say —
must be true.
Mother, who
spoke to you
out of the darkness,
out of the blue?
What did they say?
What would you do?
What could you do,
hearing those words
out of the blue?
I am a mother.
I was there, too.
I am there, too.

COMING HOME

Since I saw you last,
I went west, found a
never thought of fondness
for wild things scaling
rocky outcroppings,
sipping at snow melt
sailing far above
aspens and spruce.

Since I saw you last,
I fell in love with skies
so blue they'd make the
ocean weep
air so crisp it crackles
with each breath.

Since I saw you last,
I tasted sweet grass on the wind
found a mirror at my feet,
combed my hair by starlight
shining up from blue green
untouched splendid moments.

Since I saw you last,
I went home in silence
to deeps and highs
beyond imagining
to jeweled hummingbirds,
Stellar's jays, nutcrackers,
to soft hills before
glacial lakes were filled
or shining mountains
ever rose to meet endless skies.

Since I saw you last,
I found the path I'd missed
in all my wandering,
the landscape of my waking dreams,
the home I'd never known
among firs and willows
by the boulder tumbled creek
in the canyon.

So I came to say
goodbye to my old friends, to you.
I will have no regret
at leaving this place
where I have sojourned,
flat lands, flat rivers,
on my way home.
I will not miss these empty streets
ghost-filled houses
in that land so near the sky
that is and ever has been
truly home.

THE *SERIOUS ABOUT WRITING* PUBLISHING PACKAGE

Are you interested in publishing your fiction or non-fiction title with the prestige of an imprint? Do you want a staff of editors and designers to provide the best quality product possible? Is it important to keep your copyright and all profits from your book sales? Oh, and would you like it done in three months instead of the typical 18 months to two years required by a traditional publisher?

Look into our *Serious About Writing* package. We don't take commissions and don't give advances. We review your manuscript regardless if it's sent by you or by an agent. In exchange for an upfront, one-time fee, we make sure your work is in the best shape possible and receives the acceptance it deserves.

Here are just some of the advantages:
- Expert editing and design staff.
- Personal service throughout all aspects of the process.
- Prestige of a third-party publisher.
- Distribution to Amazon, Kindle, and other outlets.
- Creation of ISBN & bar code.
- Retention of all copyrights.
- One hundred percent royalties.
- Completion and publication within 90 days.
- A marketing plan that can be implemented by the author.

You can choose multiple avenues to accomplish these same tasks, or take advantage of the *Serious About Writing* package. Contact us for more information at woodenpantspub@gmail.com. You can also visit our website, woodenpantspub.com, and fill out the form on the Publication page. We look forward to working with you toward your goal of author entrepreneurship!

www.ingramcontent.com/pod-product-compliance
Lightning Source LLC
Chambersburg PA
CBHW061936290426
44113CB00025B/2928